POCKET BRAIN TEASERS

If you would like to order other fun books for kids from Robert Davies Publishing, please send us a postcard with your name and address and we will be happy to mail you our catalogue:

Robert Davies Publishing,
P.O. Box 702, Outremont, Quebec, Canada H2V 4N6

POCKET BRAIN TEASERS

by Robert Larin
Illustrations by Nicole Sarrazin-Blondin
Translated from French by Madeleine Hébert

Robert Davies Publishing
MONTREAL-TORONTO

To order this book call 1-514-933-5568
or FAX 1-514-937-8765
(USA: General Distribution Services,
Toll-free 1-800-805-1083)

ISBN 1-895854-24-5
1   2   1994   1995   1996

To Sandra Bergeron Larin,
with all my affection.

Table of contents

Introduction

All too often, math class is a time for students to let their thoughts drift elsewhere. Boredom follows quickly on the heels of disinterest, and young minds readily wander to thoughts of other places, other subjects, weekend parties or upcoming vacations. In any event, for many students, mathematics remains an unknown country with mysterious ways, a large, daunting question mark.

This little book is an invitation to the pleasure that comes from solving problems, or more precisely, from solving brain-teasers whose answers, if not always evident, are often amusing, quirky, and, what kids love most, *just plain fun*. Solving an enigma implies rising to a challenge, looking at a problem in ways different from the rote approach which is too often required of young minds when classical mathematics problems are set in classical ways in the classroom. And yet, a playful approach to learning can stimulate that rarest and most precious of all qualities, *curiosity*, and help to nurture the desire to learn. This is the approach I have taken in my book, and while the brain-teasers appeal to the reader's imagination, the setting of each problem is down-to-earth. Children are not theoreticians, and as much as they are turned on by letting their imagination take flight, they don't like dry numbers and theorems that have little to do with their own everyday world.

I hope that these pocket brain teasers will help kids to discover that we can reason in different ways, that the solution to real problems in real life often requires thinking in new and unusual ways. The road less travelled is often the shortest distance between a question and its answer, or *answers*. Stereotypes and cliché responses are not welcome in my book, nor in my world. In place of memorizing the right answer, it is wise to favour the more active mental skills of attention, clarity of reading, thoughtful non-linear cognition and the power of the imagination. The clear understanding of the question often leads to its solution. These puzzles are made for young minds of all ages, who like logic and who like to have fun. The solutions at the end of the book may not be the *only* right ones, so use your imagination, and if you find others, please let me know (you can write to me at the publisher's address on page 2).

1.

Auntie Alice is fifty years old. How many birth days does she have?

2.

Can Borderline Billy, now living in Canada, be buried in the U.S.A.?

3.

Famous explorer Alberta Arnold died on one of her last three trips to Brazil, Siberia and Pago-Pago. On which trip did she die?

4.

In National League baseball, how many outs are there in an inning?

5.

Mr. Izzy Awinner and Mrs. Shihaza Chance play five chess matches. They each win the same number of games, and there are no draws recorded. How can this be?

6.

Sinbad the Shepherd owns one hundred sheep. How many does he have left after he decides to sell fifty of them?

7.

How many animals of each species did Moses of the Old Testament take on board the Ark?

8.

Does the law allow Harry Hopeful to marry his widow's sister?

9.

How far can Robin Hood go into Sherwood Forest?

10.

Hilton Hunter only has one match. He enters a cabin in the woods for shelter and discovers a wood stove, an oil burner and a gas lamp. What should Hilton light first?

11.

30 centimeters separate each of six rungs on a ladder attached to the gunwhale of a boat. If the water level is at the first rung, and the tide is coming in and rising at 30 centimeters an hour, how long will it take for the water to reach the top rung?

12.

Cross out five letters in the following word to get a big surprise:

FAIBVIEGLSEUTRTPERRISSE

13.

Two girls have the same parents, were born at the same hour of the same day in the same month, and yet they are not twins? Can you say why?

14.

Marco and Paulo are going on a super automobile vacation: 60,000 kilometers. To prepare, they put four new tires on their car, each guaranteed for 15,000 km. Are they sure of finishing their trip without tire problems?

15.

Which English word is invariably pronounced wrong by Math teachers?

16.

What is the logical opposite of the statement "not here"?

17.

Say out loud in words in just one breath: 8,234,567.19!

18.

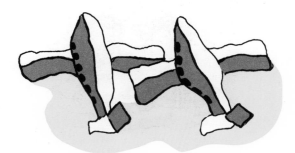

If one Airbus takes six and one half hours to cross the Atlantic Ocean, how long will it take two Airbuses?

19.

A sign on the door of the Barber of Seville says "I shave all those and only those who don't shave themselves". Does the barber also shave himself?

20.

Speaking of barbers, two of them live and work in Beardburg. One has a great haircut, the other's hair is a royal mess. A math teacher on vacation nearby needs a haircut. To which barber should he go?

21.

A train leaves the station and immediately enters a long tunnel. Where is the best seat in the train for a claustrophobic passenger?

22.

Larry the long-distance runner timed himself, and found that he ran 20 km in 80 minutes with a blue shirt on, and 20 km in one hour and twenty minutes with a red shirt on? What does this mean for his training?

23.

Which clock works best; the one that loses one minute a day, or the one that doesn't work at all?

24.

Patricia Permutate says that if a die comes up on the six five times in a row, the chances of it coming up on the next throw are very slim. Can you calculate the probability of that occurrence?

25.

Jason was thrilled to find his name on his mom's calendar. Can you figure it out?

26.

Melody LaDiva named her first children Dominique, Regis, Michelle, Fawn, Sophie and Lara. Another child is on the way. Will it be named Agatha, Shirley, Rachel or Tilly?

27.

Can you figure this one?

READING

28.

Try this one at breakfast time!

FUNEM? SVFM! FUNEX? SVFX. OK ILFMNX!

29.

Three birds are perched on an old oak branch. How many remain if a hunter shoots one of them?

30.

Rose and Violet Flower-Power have the same parents, and were born at the same hour of the same day of the same month in the same year. And *they* are not twins! Why?

31.

What's worse than a giraffe with a sore throat?

32.

I can't stand using my car for nothing. So I walk to work, walk to the supermarket, but drive to see my closest neighbour. Why would I do that?

33.

Unusual Ulric was born during winter. But in his birthday month we celebrate both the American and Canadian national holidays. What's going on here?

34.

Can you find a word that's often used in mathematics, starting with an L, ending with a C and with a G in the middle?

35.

How many tons of cod liver oil are found in an adult blue whale?

36.

Mrs Prissyprude is horrified to find a fly in her cup of tea at the restaurant. The waiter removes the cup and returns with another, only to have her exclaim: "You rotter, you brought back the same cup of tea"! It *was*, but how did she know?

37.

The Cretan philosopher Epimenides who lived in the sixth century was famous for his statement that "all Cretans are liars". Can we believe him... logically?

38.

M1ICLHLAINOCEN???

...to figure this out!

39.

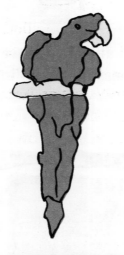

Orna Thologist is very miffed because the parrot she bought refuses to speak. The salesman assured her when she bought it that the bird always repeats what it hears. And he didn't lie. What's the explanation here?

40.

Can you find at least two ways of using a barometer to measure a building's height ?

41.

If you are waiting to take the elevator from the second floor to the top floor of a twelve-story building, chances are that the first elevator to stop at your floor will be coming down, not up. Can you think why?

42.

Many, many more people die in their beds than in car accidents. Does this mean that your bed is more dangerous than an automobile?

43.

What do these messages mean?

a)TTTTTTTTT9.9

b)$\frac{111111}{TIME}$

c)Give me a ^{5}!

44.

$$1 \times 2 \times 3 = ????$$
$$3 \times 2 \times 1 = ????$$
$$???????$$
$$!$$

If a hole is one meter deep, two meters wide and three meters long, how much earth does it contain?

45.

When Olympic diver Pavel Plunger climbed out of the pool after a perfect dive, there wasn't a wet hair on his head. How could that be?

46.

What do you have left if you cut a peach in two and give two of your friends a half each?

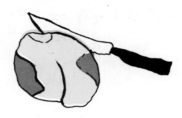

47.

Three pennies in a row. Can you think of a way to change the position of the one in the middle without touching it?

48.

If three hens lay three eggs in three days, will six hens lay six eggs in six days?

49.

A chartered airplane carrying all Canadian passengers crashes over the U.S.A. Where should the survivors be buried?

50.

W O R D   GAMES

Which word in the English language becomes shorter when it is lengthened?

51.

How many apples will you have if you take away two of the above three?

52.

Write in figures "eleven hundred eleven million eleven hundred eleven thousand eleven hundred eleven."

53.

What is the meaning of this?

HOU / SE

54.

The ancient Greek goddess Diana the huntress sent nine rabbits to her cook Anna, along with this note: "Anna, here are IX rabbits, please prepare a feast". The messenger was a thief, and stole the best three, changing the note without erasing a letter. No one was the wiser. How did he do it?

55.

If a chicken with two legs goes 4 meters in a minute and a sheep with four legs goes 8 meters in a minute, how many legs does a horse that goes 16 meters in a minute have?

56.

Doctor Feelgood gave three pills to his patient, George McSwallow, and told him to take one every half hour. How long will the cure take?

57.

I have some change in my pocket. However, even though I have $1.15 in all, I can't make change for a dollar, or 50 cents, or a quarter, dime or a nickel. Can you determine exactly what change I have?

58.

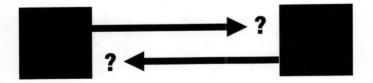

The following sentence is false." "The preceding sentence is true." Are these two sentences true or are they false?

59.

Which weighs more, 1 kilogram of lead or 1 kilogram of feathers?

60.

"There are exactly eight words in this sentence." This statement is obviously true. Find one that says exactly the opposite while still remaining true.

61.

Goody Samaritan gives someone $1. Goody is this person's brother, but this person is not Goody's brother. How can this be?

62.

A statistician gives a mathematics test to everyone in a village of six thousand inhabitants, and at the same time measures their foot size. He finds that in general, math ability rises along with the length of a person's feet. How can you explain this?

63.

You are driving a bus which can carry 48 junior high school students aged between 12 and thirteen. Can you determine the age of the bus driver?

64.

A hunter is 100 meters south of a bear. He walks 100 meters east, aims his rifle due north, and shoots the bear. What colour does the bear have to be?

65.

"A good car doesn't come cheap." "Cheap cars aren't good." Do both of these sentences say the same thing?

66.

How many times does 4 cm go into 8 dollars?

67.

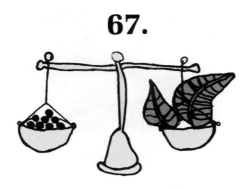

Which weighs more: 1 dm^3 of lead or 1 dm^3 of feathers?

68.

Melanie reads everything she can lay her hands on. One evening, just as she was finishing a new detective novel, there was an electrical power outage. But she was able to finish reading anyway. Do you know why?

69.

Marvin the sleepy mathematician went to bed at ten o'clock and set his alarm clock for noon. How many hours did he sleep before the alarm clock rang?

70.

Speaking of time, a grandfather clock rings six times in five seconds. How many times will it ring in ten seconds?

71.

If a rabbit that weighs about 2 pounds eats 1 kilogram of carrots a week, about how much will it weigh at the end of the year?

72.

What colour was Napoleon's white horse?

73.

What does this mean?

I 1 2 B A P

74.

If man descended from the apes, and the apes came down from the trees, can we say that man descended from the trees?

75.

If I organize a lottery in a class of 32 students, and I pick the winning number to be between 1 and 25, can I be sure that there will be at least one winner?

76.

The result of multiplying three prime numbers between six and fifteen inspired one of the world's best-known books. Can you find which one?

77.

A farmer has 17 sheep. They all died, but 9. How many does he have left, if any?

78.

If a piece of string measures one meter long at one o'clock, how long will it be at three o'clock?

79.

Patty made some punch for the party, using one cup of wine and four cups of juice. Peter made some too, with three cups of wine and twelve cups of juice. The question is, which punch tastes more "winey"?

80.

Mrs. Magoo has three daughters. They each have two brothers. But how many kids does Mrs. Magoo have in all?

81.

Statistics prove that most car accidents take place close to home. Are we safer when we are far away from home?

82.

The pet circus is looking for a new animal trainer. Should it hire Alfie who trained his dog to sing or Amanda who trained her cat to speak?

83.

All comedians are artists. Some artists are loved by their public. Can we say then, that at least some comedians are loved by their public?

84.

ACHIEVER	
AN	

HIGHLY	
CONFIDENT	

What expressions are hidden in each of the above squares?

85.

Ivan Hoe and his daughter Calamity Jane have a terrible car accident. The father dies and his daughter is gravely injured. The surgeon at the hospital looks at the girl and asks a colleague to operate, saying that "Calamity is my daughter". Can you explain?

86.

Is a half-full glass of lemonade more empty or more full than a half-empty glass?

87.

Prudence and Innocence Jailbird are tried for murder. The jury finds one innocent, the other guilty. Why does the judge free them both?

88.

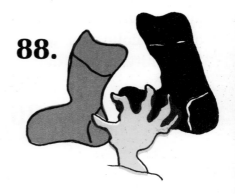

I have twelve red socks and twelve black socks in my dresser drawer. If the lights are off, how many socks must I take out, at a minimum, to be sure that I have at least one pair the same colour?

89.

Jackson Explorer is condemned to death by running a gauntlet in a strange land. He has to choose between a room full of horrible fires, a room with twenty assassins armed to the teeth, and a room with five lions that haven't eaten in ten years. If he wants to survive, which room should he choose?

90.

Robert was born in 1970. He was ten in 1980 and was in fifth grade. The sum of these numbers is 3965. Sylvie was born in 1965. She was 15 in 1980 and was in fifth level secondary school. Her total is also 3965. Is this pure chance?

91.

Seven people go into a restaurant. But there is only one table free, with six chairs. The first person sits down, and the second sits on his lap. The third one takes the second chair, the fourth, the third chair, the fifth, the fourth chair and the sixth, the fifth chair. The person sitting on the first person takes the last chair. How did seven people succeed in sitting on six chairs?

92.

What's the difference between a dollar and a half and thirty five-cents?

93.

Nelson Nabob, the head of a supermarket chain, passes by his office on the way to the airport, to get some important documents. The night watchman sees him at his desk and says, "Please, sir, don't take that flight, I just dreamt you died in a plane crash." Superstitious Nelson takes the train and learns the plane did indeed crash. Upon returning, he gives his employee a big reward and then fires him. Why is he such an ingrate?

94.

What is the most change I can have in my pocket and still be unable to make change for a dollar?

95.

Simple Simon was hired to decorate his best friend's apartment. He botched the job, and decided to ask the advice of his priest. When he left the confession box, what did he do?

96.

Since there are more people on the face of the earth than hairs on any one person's head, can we conclude that there are at least two people on the earth with exactly the same number of hairs on their head?

97.

Four workers take five days to redo the roof of a ten-story building. How many days would eight workers have taken if the building was twice as high?

98.

The day before yesterday, Alvin was 18. Next year he'll be 21. But *how*, you say, can this be?

99.

Will you answer "no" to this question?

100.

In any one year, how many months have 28 days?

101.

A big badger and a little badger are basking in the sun. The little badger is the daughter of the big badger, but the big badger isn't the mother of the little one. Do you know why?

102.

Divide 30 by 1/2 and add ten. What do you get?

103.

Harry Horsefly was a frequent flyer. Scared by the idea of a terrorist attack, he always kept a dud bomb in his suitcase, thinking it was improbable for two bombs to turn up on the same plane. Was he right?

104.

Psychiatrist Izzie Conshus was head of a mental institution who often gave lie detector tests to his patients to determine if they should be discharged. One patient, to the question "Are you Napoleon?" anwered "no", but the machine said he lied. Should he be discharged?

105.

What is the meaning of

$$\frac{1}{8}?$$

106.

Two coins together make thirty cents. The first isn't a quarter. What are the two coins?

107.

An archeologist discovers an old coin dated 44 B.C. "This coin is fake" he says. How does he know?

108.

Hilda and Keith find a metal pipe sticking up from the ground with a ping-pong ball down at the bottom. How can they get it out?

109.

What was the biggest island in the world before the discovery of Australia by Captain Cook?

110.

Several coins are placed in a row. There is one coin in the middle, two coins in front of a coin and two coins behind a coin. What is the minimum number of coins you need to make this work?

111.

Liverpool Lenny says to his friend No Account, "I'll bet you a dollar that if you give me a fiver I'll give you back ten." Is this a smart bet? For who?

112.

If a bicycle is attached to a fence with four pickets, and a four-wheel wagon is attached to fence with eight pickets, how many wheels would a tricycle attached to a fence with ten pickets have?

113.

A rubber ball is tossed off the top of a 32 meter building. Each time it hits the ground it bounces back halfway. How many times will it bounce before it comes to rest?

114.

Two gamblers decide to settle a bet by throwing three dice. The first gambler throws a "twelve" and proclaims himself the winner. What do you think?

115.

Can you duplicate this arrangement of matches by taking away three and adding only two others?

116.

What does this mean?

LNZ2CC: "$\dfrac{I1118BBBB}{CCCCCCCC}$";

CCZ:"EE-E!"

117.

Cedric Small Fry observed that his six hens lay six eggs in six days. He wants to know how many hens he would need to get one hundred eggs in one hundred days. Can you help him out?

118.

Gillian Greenhorn the explorer met a native on one of her trips, who told her that there were no more cannibals in his tribe because the last one was eaten at the previous evening meal. What should she think of his story?

119.

Why did the centipede arrive late for his appointment with the insect psychiatrist?

120.

Ivar Emedi, the male nurse, decided to leave his patient Weaken Tired in peace and not awaken him for his medecine. Why would a nurse do that?

121.

Do you need a minibus to transport four fathers, two grand-dads and four sons?

Answers

1. Just one. Auntie Alice, like you and me and everybody else, was only born once!

2. No, because nobody who is alive *anywhere* can be legally buried!

3. The *last* one! (Unless you count the trip to the cemetery!)

4. In the National League and in every other league in baseball, there are six outs in an inning, and only three per *half*-inning.

5. They play five games *each*, all right, but not against each *other.*

6. One hundred. He has only *decided* to sell them. The sheep haven't been sold yet.

7. None. In the Old Testament, *Noah*, not Moses, had the Ark.

8. No, it won't, because if he has a *widow*, he's already *dead*, and dead men can't legally get married!

9. Robin can go *in* to the forest to its centre; after that, he starts to come *out.*

10. Hilton, if he's smart, will decide that the first thing he should light is…the match!

11. It will take forever, because if the *water* rises, so will the *boat,* and the *ladder.* It would be different if the ladder was attached to the side of a dock.

12. *A big surprise.*

13. They were not born in the same year.

14. No. They are sure of going only 15,000 km without problems.

15. *Wrong.* It's always pronounced that way, even by Math teachers.

16. Here.

17. Eight million two hundred thirty-four thousand five hundred sixty-seven point nineteen.

18. Six and one half hours. They both have to cross the same ocean!

19. The British philosopher and mathematician Lord Bertrand Russell created this paradox. If the barber shaves *himself,* he contradicts his sign. If he *doesn't* shave himself, he also contradicts his sign. There is no logical solution to this paradox concerning groups.

20. The logical math teacher will go straight to the barber with the *bad* hair cut, since he cut the hair of the *other* barber, whose hair is well trimmed.

21. The best seat is the last one in the train. Since the train accelerates when leaving the station, the last seat on the last car will pass through the tunnel in the least time.

22. It means he should remember that eighty minutes is the same thing as one hour twenty minutes!

23. Lewis Caroll, the author of *Alice in Wonderland*, solved this puzzle. The clock that loses one minutes a day will give the right time again when it will have lost twelve hours (720 minutes), ie in 720 days. The other clock is better: it gives the right time twice a day.

24. One in six. The die has no memory of former results, and each toss is independent of the last.

25. He looked at the last half of the year and found **J**uly, **A**ugust, **S**eptember, **O**ctober and **N**ovember!

26. Tilly, because Melody loves music and named her children for the notes of the scale: Do, Re, Mi, Fa, So, La… Ti

27. Reading between the lines!

28. Have you any ham? Yes we have ham. Have you any eggs? Yes we have eggs. OK. I'll have ham and eggs.

29. None. The others fly off.

30. Rose and Violet are either siamese, or born the same day in a different week of the month, or they have other brothers or sisters born with them and so are triplets, quadruplets, etc.

31. A centipede with bunions.

32. His friend works in a drive-in movie.

33. Ulric was born in the Southern Hemisphere, where July falls in Winter.

34. LOGIC

35. None. You might look in a cod, if you can still find one.

36. She had put sugar in her tea before she saw the fly.

37. This is another paradox. Like the barber, the liar makes a statement that contains an internal contradiction. This paradox astonished the ancient Greeks who couldn't believe that a sensible sentence could be neither true nor false without contradicting itself. Chrysippa the stoic was said to have written no less than six treatises on this paradox; unfortunately, none have come down to us. Also, St. Paul alludes to this in his epistle to Titus I, 12-13.

38. One chance in a million. (M1ICLHLAINOCEN)

39. The parrot is deaf.

40. In addition to the obvious solution of measuring the air pressure at the bottom and the top, you could bribe the janitor with the barometer to tell you the building's height, or let the barometer fall to earth from the top of the building and measure the time it took to hit the ground ($h = 1/2 \, gt^2$). Other solutions are also possible.

41. There is only one chance that the elevator cage is on the ground floor going up, but ten chances that is is ony any of the third to twelfth floors going down. The chances are 10 in 11, or about 90%.

42. No. Go back to sleep.

43. a) 99.9.   b) Once upon a time.   c)Give me a high five.

44. None. It's empty.

45. He is bald.

46. The pit.

47.

48. No. If three hens lay three eggs in three days, they lay one egg each day. Six hens will lay two eggs per day and six eggs in three days. In *six* days they will lay *twelve* eggs.

49. Survivors, as a general rule, are not buried!

50. Short.

51. Two.

52. 1,112,112,111

53. A divided house.

54. The crooked messenger added an S in front of the IX, and the cook thought there were only six rabbits. Diana wasn't too pleased at the lack of food at her feast and this gave rise to the old saying "If you don't like the message, kill the messenger".

55. Four.

56. One hour. George takes the first pill, waits thirty minutes, takes the second pill, and when he takes the last pill thirty minutes later, only one hour has passed in all.

57. A fifty-cent piece, a quarter and four dimes.

58. This again is a paradox, because if the first sentence is true, then the second is false, which makes the first false also! If the first sentence is false, by the same reasoning, the second being true, the first must be true, but...

59. They both weigh the same : 1 kilogram.

60. The number of words in this sentence is not equal to eleven.

61. The someone is his sister.

62. Since "everyone in the village" includes babies and children, and childrens' feet are small but grow as they learn and grow older, the average math ability in the village seems to rise with foot length, or age.

63. Yes, since the driver is yourself.

64. White, since it is a polar bear (if not, the hunter wouldn't be aiming North when he shoots — it would be northwest, northeast, etc.)

65. From a logical point of view, both sentences are the equivalent of "There are no cars which are both good *and* cheap." Psychologically, the first sentence suggests a car good and expensive, while the second suggests a cheap but mediocre automobile.

66. No times. There are no centimeters in a dollar.

67. Since we are talking about equal volumes, it is obvious that one tenth of a cubic meter of lead weighs more that one tenth of a cubic meter of feathers.

68. Melanie is blind, and while it is literally true that "she reads everything she can lay her hands on," the presence or absence of light has no effect on her reading in braille.

69. Unless it was a digital or electric clock, it would ring at midnight (12:00) and he would get only *two hours* of shuteye.

70. Eleven times. The ringing starts at 0 seconds, and then rings ten times, ending at the tenth ring, at exactly the tenth second.

71. Just about 1 kilogram, because that is what little rabbits weigh.

72. White!

73. I WANT TO BE HAPPY!

74. No. These statements are not logically linked and have no connection to each other. Except that any human, like any ape, can descend from a tree if he or she is already sitting in it!

75. No. Any number of people could choose numbers from 26 to 32, in which nobody would win and your classmates would not find your game much fun.

76. Prime numbers are divisible only by themselves and the number 1. The only prime numbers between 6 and 15 are 7, 11 and 13, and multiplied together they make 1001: the famous *1001 Nights* or *Sheharazade*.

77. He has nine left. Read the problem again!

78. One meter, unless it's alive and growing. But this is a very rare occurence with string!

79. Both punches taste the same, since the proportions are the same: 1/4 and 3/12.

80. Five children : three girls and two boys.

81. Of course not! But since we drive more often closer to our homes, we are more likely to have accidents closer to our homes.

82. Alfie, because since cats can't speak, Amanda is a *ventriloquist*, not an animal trainer.

83. Not necessarily, since as this figure shows, *all* the comedians could be a part of the *some* of the artists not loved by their public.

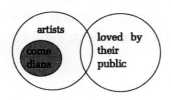

84. A) an underachiever; B) highly over-confident

85. The surgeon is Calamity's mother.

86. A half-full glass and a half-empty glass both are equally full and equally empty.

87. They are siamese twins, and the judge can't imprison the guilty one without also imprisoning the innocent one.

88. Three. With three socks you can be sure that either they will all be the same colour, or one will be different. In either case you'll have a same-colour pair. Thirteen is the number of socks to take to be sure of having at least two different colour socks, and fourteen to have a same colour pair of a *particular* colour.

89. The third room. Lions that haven't eaten in ten years are dead.

90. Not at all. 3965 is twice 1980 plus 5. 1980 plus the sum of any two years which add up to 1980 (1970 plus 10 for Robert, 1965 plus 15 for Sylvie) is the same as twice 1980. The statements are the same, to which we added 5 in each case, and this results in 3965 for both.

91. They didn't. We told you that the person *sitting on the first chair* takes the last chair, but that still leaves the *seventh* person, who hasn't been mentioned. He eats standing up. I bet you do that a lot, too!

92. None. A dollar and a half is the same as thirty five-cents. (But not the same as thirty-five *cents!*)

93. The night watchman was sleeping on the job.

94. $1.19. One quarter, nine dimes and four pennies; *or,* three quarters, four dimes and four pennies, *or* one fifty-cent piece, one quarter, four dimes and four pennies.

95. Re-paint. (Repent)

96. Yes. There are certainly at least two completely bald people with no hair at all. But even if there were less people on the face of the earth than hairs on anybody's head, there still could be two people with the same number of hairs. The second proposition is thus always true, and not a conclusion of the first.

97. Two days and a half: the height of the building has no pertinence here, only the number of workers.

98. Alvin was born on the 31st of december, and the statement was made on January 1. The day before yesterday is thus December 30, and Alvin was 18. *Yesterday* he was 19. This coming December 31 he will be 20, and *next year* (on December 31) he will be 21.

99. Another paradox. You cannot say yes or no without contradicting yourself.

100. All of them: i.e. 12.

101. The big badger is the little badger's *father.*

102. Seventy. Not to be confused with "divide 30 by 2 and add ten," which would give 25. Dividing by a half is the same as multiplying by 2.

103. No. The probability of their being a dud bomb has no link to the probability of their being a live bomb on board. Harry should take the train.

104. Since lie detectors don't always work, and the psychiatrist should know that Napoleon is no longer with us, he should let his patient go.

105. I over-ate

106. The first coin is a nickel, and the *second*, a quarter.

107. Because B.C. (before Christ) was not used until *after* the birth of Christ. A coin can't be dated with reference to a date after it supposedly was struck.

108. They pour water into the pipe, and the ping-pong ball floats out.

109. Australia was always the biggest island in the world, even *before* it was discovered by Captain Cook.

110. Three.

111. It's a good bet for Lenny. He gets five from his "mark" and only has to give back one, to pay his lost wager. Don't gamble!

112. Three. A tricycle always has only three wheels.

113. In theory, an awful long time. Think of the series of bounces: 32, 16, 8, 4, 2, 1, 1/2, then 1/4, 1/8, 1/16, 1/32, 1/64 and so on. That would be in a gravity-free environment. But on the earth, gravity will eventually cause it to stop bouncing.

114. He'd better wait and see what his opponent throws. With *three* dice, he could through a score up to 18. 12 is the maximum with *two* dice.

115. Take away three matchsticks and place them like this:

| | |

then add the two others to *these* sticks, not to the first ones, to complete the pattern:

| | | | |.

116. Helen said to Sissy, "I once ate four bees overseas; Sissy said, "too easy".

117. Six. If six hens lay six eggs in six days, they together lay one egg each day and Cedric will need the same six hens to lay one hundred eggs in…one hundred days.

118. Miss Greenhorn should ask herself who ate the last cannibal, before she turns into someone's dinner herself!

119. A sign on the door asked visitors to wipe their feet before coming in.

120. The medecine was a sleeping pill.

121. No, because to carry two kids, each with their dad and their grandpa, you only need a regular-sized car.

Classroom Tips

Teaching math and logic

No learning is worthwhile unless the knowledge acquired is clearly significant and thus more easily assimilated. The teaching of mathematics, in my opinion, should be aimed less at the acquisition of skills and more at helping the student to really understand the concepts that lie behind the immediate problem at hand. And this is really where our weakness as teachers often lies. Mathematics in the classroom, even today, revolves mainly around ideas which are presented as theorems, recipes to be rigorously applied without much thinking. Unfortunately, by teaching this way we keep students' understanding at the level of magic! Things happen without the student *understanding* , and mathematics becomes an inaccessible and esoteric subject.

In my own classes I often meet with students' resistance when I try to address their cognitive abilities (to help them discover ways of thinking) rather than to their ability to execute (in the demonstration of algorithms to be applied). They have been so "well trained" that for them, mathematics is nothing more than some rote sets of rules to be used to arrive at solutions, tricks that they have already learned and which, more often than not, they don't even apply correctly! They believe that a good math teacher, one who teaches "properly," has only to teach the right formulas which, when applied at the appropriate moment with little cognitive input, obtain the "right" answer to the "right" question. Sadly enough, some people call this reflex programming "learning" mathematics.

I feel that the road to a solution of this pedagogical curse goes through a different way of approaching problem-solving. I would like to see a methodology of teaching put into practise that as much as possible takes account of the following two principles:

1) *In elementary school, fewer actual mathematical concepts should be taught. Instead, the emphasis should be placed on exploring and discovering more by solving various puzzles and logic problems of different kinds.*

Too many facts are taught in elementary school, and the students just don't have the time to assimilate the plethora of details. Over and above counting and basic mathematical operations, which must be taught, we should try instead to motivate students to enjoy problem solving by confronting them with a wide variety of problems *including* mathematics problems. This kind of an approach tends to put all the little pieces of information together into a comprehensible whole and pedagogically speaking, it is much more sound.

If we could limit ourselves to fostering a taste for discovery, developing the pleasure of conducting research for its own sake, nurturing the joy of exploration and finding results oneself, then the understanding and application of mathematics in later grades would certainly reside on much firmer ground. During high school, students would be able to more easily acquire complex mathematical notions and use them intuitively, without the handicap of mental fog, and retain that knowledge much longer in their lives for the simple reason that they would actually *understand*.

2) *The teaching of problem resolution should not be solely mathematical in nature, but multidisciplinary.* I find that secondary-level students all too often give up on fairly simple problems and hide behind the old line about not having a head for figures. Down comes the curtain, and the student's mind becomes a brick wall that no further attempts at communication can penetrate. But in fact, we should encourage

children right from elementary school to know that in life, these kinds of difficulties are a natural and absolutely normal part of the process of discovery. If we understand the problem right from the start, it isn't much of a problem. The fun becomes a mental game of seeing just how hard it will be to find a solution. And obviously, this approach of allowing the students to find their way to the solutions means giving them enought time to:

1- explore the problem and its description;

2- navigate through their creative processes to imagine various hypotheses and solutions;

3 - evaluate in groups the various solutions proposed and choose one which the seems to be the most promising;

4 - write down an acceptable presentation;

5 - evaluate and comment on the process.

This is a multi-disciplinary approach, and it also has the advantage of favoring both individual and group activities.

This book was never intended to be only a collection of mathematical brain-teasers. There are already many excellent books which are just that, and only that. My aim was to distract and amuse the young readers of this book, to capture their minds for while in a first-pass approach to the methods of solving problems. Without making my intentions too ambitious, I also wanted to make a modest contribution to helping prepare my readers, while they play at brain-teasers, to experience the kind of multiple complex problems that, in the future, they will face in their own lives. All too soon, moreover.